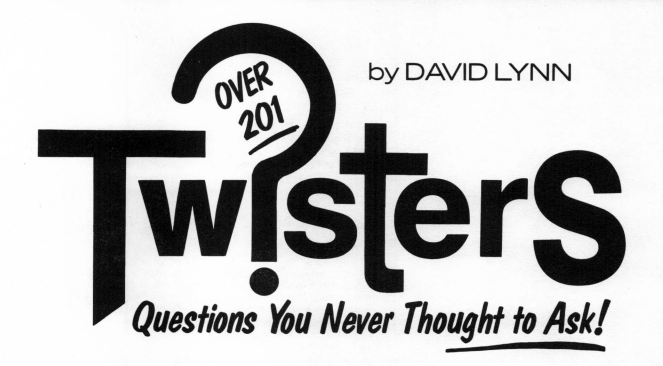

by DAVID LYNN

OVER 201

Tw?sterS

Questions You Never Thought to Ask!

Lamplighter Books Grand Rapids, Michigan
Zondervan Publishing House

TWISTERS
Copyright © 1990 by David Lynn

Lamplighter Books is an imprint of The Zondervan Publishing House
1415 Lake Drive, S.E., Grand Rapids, Michigan 49506

Library of Congress Cataloging-in-Publication Data

Lynn, David, 1954—
     Twisters : questions you never thought to ask / David Lynn.
          p.   cm.
     ISBN 0-310-52262-5 (paper)
     1. Christian life—Miscellanea. 2. Conduct of life—Miscellanea. I. Title.
BV4517.L95   1990
248—dc20   90–38207
                                                                CIP

Edited by John Sloan, Jack Kuhatschek
Designed by Rachel Hostetter
Cover art and interior illustrations by Michael Streff

Printed in the United States of America

90 91 92 93 94 95 / AK / 10 9 8 7 6 5 4 3 2 1

ACKNOWLEDGMENTS

Many thanks to Grace Barnes, Rod McKean, and Robin Smith of Azusa Pacific University and Carol Hubbard, Steve Jones, Bill Nicholson, Pat Thompson, and Wes Wesner of Casas Adobes Church for their constructive feedback.

Thanks also to Scott Bolinder and John Sloan of Zondervan for their generous assistance.

Deep thanks to my wife, Kathy, a constant source of help and encouragement. I love you!

CONTENTS

Tired of Bible trivia questions? Welcome to *Twisters*, a book packed with thought-provoking, nerve-racking, conversation-starting, laughter-generating, out-of-the-ordinary, crazy questions.

Bertrand Russell once said, "Most people would sooner die than think; in fact, they do so." If some of your friends and acquaintances fit Russell's description, wake them up with a challenging Twister.

Twisters can be used in a variety of settings—between friends, for personal reflection, in a newsletter, as a party icebreaker, during retreats, as a conversation creator, to begin a Bible study, as a Sunday school crowd breaker, or just for fun.

You are the judge of the best way to use a Twister question. If you wish to use only a Teaser or Theologizer, you can. If you want to modify a question,

INTRODUCTION

do so. If you or your group invents a question, mail it to us (see Create-A-Twister for details).

You will quickly notice that a Twister question begins with an out-of-the-ordinary grabber question. This can be followed by a Turn-A-Bout question that twists the original. A Teaser question may follow that personalizes the initial question even further or in a different way. A Theologizer does just as its name implies—it brings God intimately into the picture. Finally, there may be a Twister Plus question that piggybacks on the topic being considered.

Have fun!

TWISTER #1

Could you
or your group
create a
TWISTER

CREATE-A-TWISTER!

Invent your own Twister, and you or your group may see it published in *Twisters: The Sequel*, our second volume of out-of-the-ordinary questions.

If your Twister question is chosen and published, we will credit you or your group by printing your name or group name, city, and state on the page with your question.

Clearly print or type your question using the format seen in this book and attach it to this page or a copy of this page. Be sure to include your name and address.

NAME _____

GROUP NAME (if applicable) _____

ADDRESS _____

CITY _____ STATE _____ ZIP _____

MAIL TO:
Create-A-Twister
Zondervan Publishing House
1415 Lake Drive, S.E.
Grand Rapids, Michigan 49506

Suppose TWISTERS

TWISTER #2

Suppose you could take a test that would reveal all your character defects. How many of them would you want to know?

TURN-A-BOUT

How many of them would you want your friends to know? Your parents? Your children? Your spouse?

THEOLOGIZER

If you could hide any of your character defects from God, which would you choose to hide? Which would you reveal?

TWISTER #3

If next week were to be a high point in your spiritual life, what do you suppose would happen?

TURN-A-BOUT

How would your friends answer this question for you?

TEASER

If your spiritual cholesterol were checked, what would be discovered about your spiritual life?

THEOLOGIZER

Why would you want to be closer to God?

TWISTER PLUS

What price are you willing to pay to grow closer to God?

TWISTER #4

Suppose an amusement park ride were invented that could stimulate any human emotion. Which feeling would you choose to experience? Why?

TURN-A-BOUT

Which feelings would you not want to be stimulated?

TEASER

What do you do with feelings you do not like? What do you do with feelings you do like?

THEOLOGIZER

What feelings do you wish you could hide from God? Why?

TWISTER #5.

TURN-A-BOUT

Suppose there were an Olympic event in compassion. Could you qualify? How about integrity?

If the event were in greed, could you qualify? How about anger?

TWISTER #6.

Suppose you could keep only one book of the Bible. Which book would you choose? Why?

TURN-A-BOUT

Answer the question again, but suppose you were living in Old Testament times!

TEASER

If you were to start a personal Bible study today, where would you begin?

THEOLOGIZER

Which five books of the Bible do you believe God would rate as most important? Which five would he rate as least important?

TWISTER #7

Suppose you were to create a recipe for the perfect life. What would the ingredients list look like?

TURN-A-BOUT

What ingredients would you definitely exclude from your list?

TEASER

How closely does your life mirror your recipe?

THEOLOGIZER

If God were to create the recipe, what would it look like?

TWISTER #8

Suppose you were to become a college student tomorrow. What course of study would you most likely pursue? Why?

TURN-A-BOUT

If you were to enroll in a theological seminary tomorrow, what would you most want to learn about while there?

THEOLOGIZER

What does education do to one's faith?

TWISTER PLUS

What kind of education do you want for your children or grandchildren?

TWISTER #9

Suppose a halfway house for recovering drug addicts were being located in your neighborhood. Would you vote for or against it? What if it was a halfway house for the mentally handicapped? A home for the elderly? Pregnant teenagers?

TURN-A-BOUT

If you had a relative living in one of these homes, how might this change your views?

TEASER

In what type of halfway house or group home would you most like to work? Why?

TWISTER #10

If you had the choice, would you rather be born blind or lose your sight as an adult? Why?

TURN-A-BOUT

Would it be easier to be blind or deaf?

TEASER

Assume you are not a sighted person. What would your dream life be like?

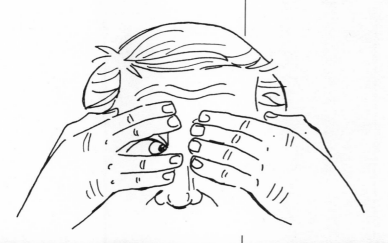

TWISTER # 11

Suppose you could change your looks. What would you want to change? What would you want to keep the same?

TURN-A-BOUT

What would your friends say needs to be changed?

THEOLOGIZER

Why do you think God created you to look the way you do?

TWISTER PLUS

Why are looks so important?

TWISTER #12

TURN-A-BOUT

If your parents knew what you thought about them, what do you suppose would surprise them the most? The least?

How will you relate to your children differently than your parents related to you?

TWISTER #13

Suppose you were a TV evangelist. What would your show look like?

TEASER

When was the last time you acted like a typical television evangelist?

THEOLOGIZER

Do you think Jesus would have used television to spread the gospel if it had been available? How about radio?

TWISTER PLUS

How have TV evangelists and radio preachers changed people's opinions of the church? Of Christianity?

TWISTER #14

THEOLOGIZER

Suppose you were allowed to write a one-paragraph letter that would be read on national television by the President of the United States. What would you say?

Suppose you were allowed to choose a passage of Scripture to be read by the President. What might you select?

TWISTER #15

Suppose you had the authority to perform weddings. What would you say or do as you officiated a wedding ceremony that was different than what others usually say or do?

TEASER

What was said at your wedding? What do you wish was said but was not?

THEOLOGIZER

What do you suppose God wishes were said or done at every wedding?

TWISTER # 16

If you were to win a state lottery worth millions of dollars, how do you suppose you would change your life? Would you change your standard of living? Would you keep the same job? Would you keep the same house? How about the same car?

TEASER

Would you want your Christian friends to know you had won?

TWISTER PLUS

How many lottery winners do you think are happier since they won?

TWISTER #17

Suppose men were the ones that had the babies. How would things be different?

TURN-A-BOUT

Answer the question again, supposing you are now a member of the opposite sex.

THEOLOGIZER

Why do you suppose God chose women to bear the children?

TWISTER #18

TURN-A-BOUT

If your best friend were seriously disfigured in a near-fatal car accident, do you suppose you would maintain your close friendship?

If it were your spouse in the accident, would you continue the marriage? Why?

TWISTER #19

TURN-A-BOUT

Suppose you could decide between attractiveness or intelligence. Which would you choose? Why?

Would you rather your best friend be more attractive or more intelligent than you? Would you rather your spouse be more attractive or more intelligent than you?

Day -to- Day TWISTERS

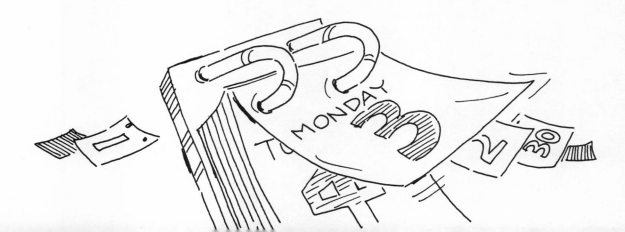

TWISTER #20

TURN-A-BOUT

What are some things that seem to clutter your life?

Are these things different now than they were ten years ago? Do you think they will still clutter your life ten years from now?

TWISTER #21

Do you give more or less money to God than the average Christian? How about time?

TEASER

If you gave more to God, would God's blessings be greater? Explain.

THEOLOGIZER

Is the ten percent tithe of the Old Testament required of today's Christian? Why or why not?

TWISTER PLUS

Is giving to the United Way giving to God?

TWISTER #22

TURN-A-BOUT

Do you see yourself as above or below average when it comes to looks? Personality? Brains? Spirituality? Self-image?

How would you rate most other people's looks? Personalities? Brains? Spirituality? Self-images?

TWISTER #23

TEASER

How immoral must a movie be for you not to watch it? How about a TV sitcom? A TV commercial? A soap opera?

Suppose you are watching a rented movie on your home VCR when a nude scene is shown. Will you turn the movie off or finish watching it to see how it ends?

TWISTER #24

THEOLOGIZER

If you could keep only three possessions you now have, what three would you choose? Why?

What material things do Christians deserve from God?

TWISTER #25

TURN-A-BOUT

TWISTER PLUS

What is one of your biggest regrets?

How have you overcome this regret?

Do you know someone who has no regrets? Is that possible?

TWISTER #26

Of the seven deadly sins—anger, lust, laziness, pride, envy, gluttony, and greed—which is least troublesome to you?

TURN-A-BOUT

Of the seven deadly sins, which is most troublesome to you?

TEASER

Think of your greatest sins. What could someone have said to you that could have prevented you from committing them?

THEOLOGIZER

When God forgives you for your sins, why do you still pay consequences for them?

Have you had more or fewer sin problems as you have grown older?

TWISTER #27

How lucky are you? Are things more likely to go right or wrong for you?

THEOLOGIZER

How does God figure into your good or bad fortune?

TWISTER #28

What decisions do you hate to make? Why?

TURN-A-BOUT

What decisions are you good at making?

THEOLOGIZER

How is God involved in your decisions?

TWISTER PLUS

What decisions have you regretted? What ones have pleased you?

TWISTER #29

How vain would others say you are?

TURN-A-BOUT

Is your gender more vain than the opposite sex? Explain.

TEASER

Suppose a topical medication were developed that guaranteed no wrinkles. Would you request a prescription even though it had to be applied daily and was quite expensive?

TWISTER PLUS

How much a slave to fashion are you?

TWISTER #30

Would you *not* spank your children if you knew they would turn out reasonably well without spankings?

TEASER

When is a child too old to spank?

THEOLOGIZER

Does God want you to spank your children? Why or why not?

TWISTER  #31

What is something you have really wanted to do but have not?

TURN-A-BOUT

What is something you did not want to do but did anyway?

THEOLOGIZER

What is one thing you have wanted to do for God but have not?

TWISTER PLUS

What do you wish you could do better?

TWISTER #32

What has the past taught us that could help us live better today or in the future?

TURN-A-BOUT

What lesson from history have we not learned and most likely will repeat?

THEOLOGIZER

What has the past taught the church? Has the church learned from its mistakes?

TWISTER PLUS

What do you think people in the future will learn from the present?

TWISTER #33

How normal are you? How normal are your friends? How about your family?

TEASER

If you could sell normality, would people buy it? Why or why not?

THEOLOGIZER

How normal is a Christian supposed to be?

TWISTER PLUS

How normal was your childhood?

TWISTER #34

TURN-A-BOUT

What is an adequate yearly income?

What size income would make you rich? What size income would keep you poor?

Faith
TWISTERS

TWISTER #35

Would you pray for thirty minutes every morning if you could be certain the practice would improve the quality of your life?

TEASER

You have been challenged to give up either television or prayer for a week. Which would be easier for you to quit for seven days?

THEOLOGIZER

Does God expect you to pray every day? At all?

TWISTER PLUS

Will God more likely answer a prayer if more people are praying? Why?

TWISTER #36

What kind of exercise would you need to get into better faith shape?

TEASER

Pretend you lived in first-century Israel and saw Christ raise the dead and heal the sick. Would this make it easier for you to live out the Christian faith?

THEOLOGIZER

Do you feel it would be easier or more difficult to have faith in God living in biblical times than living today? Why?

TWISTER #37

TURN-A-BOUT

THEOLOGIZER

What is something you like doing for others?

What is something you wish others would do for you?

What have you done for God? What has God done for you?

TWISTER #38

What would it take for you to become a missionary in a foreign country?

TURN-A-BOUT

Answer this Twister again, assuming this change would increase your present yearly income.

TEASER

Would you get rid of your household pets if it meant you could use the money saved to help support a missionary? Would you encourage your friends to follow your example?

THEOLOGIZER

Why would God want you to become a missionary in a foreign country?

TWISTER #39

Are Christians today more different or more like first-century Christians?

TURN-A-BOUT

How are you like a first-century Christian?

THEOLOGIZER

What difference is Christianity making in the church? In your church?

TWISTER #40

How spiritual do you think others think you are?

TEASER

If you were to take a test that measured spiritual growth, what kind of grade do you think you would get?

THEOLOGIZER

How would God define spirituality?

TWISTER PLUS

How do you get in the way of your own spiritual growth?

TWISTER  #41

If Christ is the answer, what questions has he answered?

TURN-A-BOUT

What questions has he not answered?

THEOLOGIZER

What about Christ or Christianity is most difficult to understand?

TWISTER PLUS

Why did Christ leave so many questions unanswered?

TWISTER #42

TURN-A-BOUT

Why do we search for the loopholes in God's commandments?

How do you tend to explain away God's commands?

TWISTER #43

TURN-A-BOUT

Christ asked his most important question to his disciples—"Who do you say I am?" (Matthew 16:15). Who do you say Christ is?

How often do you tell others who Christ is?

TWISTER #44

Would you preach the gospel on a street corner in your hometown if you knew someone would find God?

TURN-A-BOUT

Answer the question again assuming you would be paid $10,000 to preach.

THEOLOGIZER

Would Christ preach on street corners today? Do you think you would stop and listen if he did?

TWISTER PLUS

How easy do you find it to share your faith with your family? With friends? With strangers?

TWISTER # 45

Have you found what you are looking for in life?

TURN-A-BOUT

What have you found in life that you are definitely not looking for?

TEASER

If someone were to ask what happiness is, what would you most likely tell them?

THEOLOGIZER

How would you define the meaning and purpose of life to an atheist?

TWISTER PLUS

What, in your opinion, is the best way to enjoy life?

TWISTER #46

If there is, in fact, an afterlife, why do many Christians live as though this is all there is?

TURN-A-BOUT

If there were no afterlife, would someone who lived as though there were be better or worse off? Why?

THEOLOGIZER

How can you make God's perspective on life your perspective?

TWISTER PLUS

How involved in your life will you allow God to become?

TWISTER #47

Would you more likely associate the word *comfort* or the word *challenge* with your church? Why?

TEASER

Do you attend church often enough? Too often?

THEOLOGIZER

What does God expect from your church?

TWISTER PLUS

What is the biggest issue pushing Christians out of the American church?

Prediction TWISTERS

TWISTER #48

Tom Wolfe has said the twenty-first century could become the twentieth century's hangover! What consequences will America pay in the next century for this century's lifestyles?

TURN-A-BOUT | What do you think people living in the 1890s said about the twentieth century?

THEOLOGIZER | Compared to past centuries, how do you suppose God would rate the twentieth century?

TWISTER PLUS | What do you expect from the future?

TWISTER  #49

How surprised will Christians be with what they find in heaven?

TURN-A-BOUT

What might surprise you the most? The least?

TEASER

Will your friends be surprised that you will be in heaven? Why?

TWISTER #50

TURN-A-BOUT

TWISTER PLUS

Herpes was the scourge of the 1970s and AIDS of the 1980s. What direction might sexually transmitted diseases take in the 1990s?

How has the scare of sexually transmitted diseases changed your views on sexuality?

When a cure is found for AIDS, how will it affect people's sexuality?

TWISTER #51

What future scientific discovery could invalidate the Christian faith?

TURN-A-BOUT

What scientific discovery could validate the Christian faith?

TEASER

Evidence is continually being found that tends to support the theories of evolution. As more new evidence is discovered, will it damage your Christian faith? Why or why not?

TWISTER #52

Why has Christ not yet returned?

TURN-A-BOUT

Do you think Christ will return in your lifetime? Why or why not?

THEOLOGIZER

If you could be certain that Christ would return in one month, how would you live your life differently during the next four weeks?

TWISTER #53

TURN-A-BOUT

THEOLOGIZER

Do you think the world will survive until the year 2000?

If the world does survive the twentieth century, will it be a world in which you want to live?

What will be the state of the Christian church in the year 2000?

TWISTER #54

THEOLOGIZER

What is one of the first questions you will ask God when you meet face-to-face?

What is one of the first questions God might ask you when the two of you meet face-to-face?

TWISTER #55

THEOLOGIZER

How will society be different as the baby boomer generation grows older?

How will the American church change as its baby boomers age?

TWISTER #56

Do you think there will ever be a World War III?

TURN-A-BOUT

Will it include nuclear weapons?

TEASER

If nuclear weapons are used again for military purposes, how do you think the Christian community will respond?

THEOLOGIZER

Can a Christian justify a nuclear war? Why or why not?

TWISTER #57

How will the values of the average Christian change in the next ten years?

TURN-A-BOUT

In what direction would you like them to go?

THEOLOGIZER

What role will God's Word play in shaping the values of the average American Christian in the next ten years?

Inter-Generational TWISTERS

TWISTER #58

If you could be any age, what age would you choose to be? Why?

TURN-A-BOUT

How good were "the good old days"?

THEOLOGIZER

What would Jesus say were the golden years of your life?

TWISTER #59

What has been the biggest mistake your generation has made?

TURN-A-BOUT

What was the biggest mistake your parents' generation made?

THEOLOGIZER

What is the biggest error your generation has made in its relationship to God? To the church?

TWISTER #60

What do you expect out of life? What is one thing about life at your present age that you did not expect?

TURN-A-BOUT

What is one thing about life right now that you wish was not true?

THEOLOGIZER

What does God expect out of your life now?

TWISTER #61

What might be the happiest memory of your senior adult years?

TURN-A-BOUT

What might be the worst memory of your senior adult years?

THEOLOGIZER

How do you think God wants you to spend your retirement?

TWISTER #62

TURN-A-BOUT

THEOLOGIZER

How old do you wish you could live to be?

When do you think you will die?

If God were willing to tell you the exact day you would die, would you want to know? How about the cause of your death?

TWISTER #63

TURN-A-BOUT

Do you hope that life will be easier or more difficult for your children than it has been for you?

Did your parents make it too easy or too difficult for you? How?

TWISTER #64

TEASER

At your next high school reunion, will your classmates be surprised at the direction your life has taken?

You are at your next high school reunion. A close friend of yours from high school is rating how successful your classmates have become. Will she rate you as more or less successful than the average person in your high school graduating class? Why?

TWISTER #65

If you could live a day in your life over again, what day would you choose? Why?

TURN-A-BOUT

What is a day you would never choose?

THEOLOGIZER

What is a day God might wish you to relive?

TWISTER #66

What is right with today's generation of young people?

TURN-A-BOUT

What is wrong with today's generation of young people?

THEOLOGIZER

What values need to be instilled into this generation of young people?

TWISTER PLUS

What could you say to this generation of young people that would have an impact on them? What could you do to have an impact on them?

TWISTER #67

TURN-A-BOUT

If you could do it over, would you have children?

If you do not now have children, will you? Why? Do you think you will regret your decision?

Mind TWISTERS

TWISTER #68

If we ever discover life on another planet, what do you think their religious beliefs will look like? Will Jesus Christ be central to their beliefs?

TURN-A-BOUT

Do you believe we will discover life on another planet? Will it discover us?

THEOLOGIZER

What would stop God from creating rational life on another planet just as he created human beings on earth?

TWISTER #69

What is written in the Bible that you wish were not?

TURN-A-BOUT

What do you wish were written in the Bible that is not?

TEASER

How much authority does the Bible have over your life?

TWISTER #7_0

TURN-A-BOUT

THEOLOGIZER

Why do bad things happen to good people?

Why do good things happen to bad people?

How does evil touching your life change your view of life? Of God?

TWISTER #71

TURN-A-BOUT

Since children tend to be like their parents, what do you think your adult children will be like?

How are you like your parents or grandparents?

TWISTER #72

Does prayer change God's mind? Why or why not?

TURN-A-BOUT

How do you change when you pray?

THEOLOGIZER

Does God respond to the prayers of people who are not Christians?

TWISTER #73

TURN-A-BOUT

What is one thing worth dying for? Would you actually die for it?

What is one thing not worth dying for that many people are willing to die for anyway?

TWISTER #74

What are the five most important Christian beliefs?

TURN-A-BOUT

What are five unimportant Christian beliefs?

THEOLOGIZER

What Christian beliefs are worth fighting for?

TWISTER #75

THEOLOGIZER

TWISTER PLUS

Does the end justify the means if the end is motivated by love?

Could lying be considered right in certain circumstances? How about abortion? How about murder?

What moral absolutes, if any, are there?

TWISTER #76

What would happen to Christianity in America if all churches became like yours?

TEASER

You are glancing through the paper and catch a headline about your church. If you decided to read the article, what do you think it might say?

THEOLOGIZER

Would Christ want to attend your church? Why or why not?

TWISTER #77

THEOLOGIZER

TWISTER PLUS

What will happen to someone who has never heard about Christ?

How real is hell? Could a loving God really send someone to hell?

Is Jesus Christ the only way to God?

TWISTER #78

What is one of the greatest untruths you have ever heard?

TURN-A-BOUT

What is the greatest untruth you have ever believed?

THEOLOGIZER

What is truth?

Tension TWISTERS

TWISTER #79

The Russians have launched a full-scale nuclear attack on the United States. Suppose you were the only person who could give the signal to launch a counterattack. Knowing that America was already doomed, would you push the button anyway, insuring the destruction of the Soviet Union?

TEASER

If you had been President of the United States at the end of World War II, would you have opposed or favored dropping the atomic bomb on Japan? Explain.

THEOLOGIZER

Is it a sin to build a nuclear weapon?

TWISTER PLUS

Can a "just" nuclear war be waged?

TWISTER #80

A large corporation offers you a "golden opportunity" job. Before taking the job, you hear about the company's poor environmental record. Do you take the job anyway?

TURN-A-BOUT

Would you take the job if the environmental problems created by the corporation were in a Third World country?

THEOLOGIZER

How accountable will God hold employees for the sins of a corporation?

TWISTER #81

TURN-A-BOUT

Your teenage son refuses to attend church, saying he has outgrown religion. What should you do?

What should you definitely not do?

TWISTER #82

Your spouse has confessed that he or she is having an affair. Do you leave your spouse or stay and work it out?

TURN-A-BOUT

If you were the one having the affair, would you confess it to your spouse?

THEOLOGIZER

Is an affair ever justifiable?

TWISTER #83

TURN-A-BOUT

You notice a neighbor's daughter climbing out her bedroom window late one weekend evening. What will you do?

If it were your daughter climbing out her bedroom window, would you want to be told? Why or why not?

TWISTER #84

You have an agreement to buy a friend's car. You find a better deal on another vehicle. Do you back out of your previous agreement? Why or why not?

TWISTER #85

If your son (or daughter) were to announce he (or she) is a homosexual, how do you think you would respond?

TEASER

How would you respond if your church announced it would be accepting practicing homosexuals for membership?

THEOLOGIZER

What is it about homosexuality that God condemns?

TWISTER #86

A family in your neighborhood is having a moving sale, having lost their home to fore- closure. Knowing of their financial difficulties, would you offer less money for their VCR than it was worth? Why or why not?

TWISTER #87

You notice your 14-year-old daughter's diary lying open on her bed. Do you read it?

TURN-A-BOUT

If you had kept a diary during your early adolescent years, would you want your children to read it now?

TWISTER PLUS

How much privacy do children deserve?

TWISTER #88

A colleague's frequent off-color jokes about women appear to offend a female employee, but she says very little. What will you say, if anything?

TURN-A-BOUT

If the jokes were racist in nature, would you say anything?

TWISTER #89

You find out one of your favorite food brands is owned by a company that supports apartheid through its economic ties with South Africa. Do you continue to purchase that brand of food?

TWISTER #90

THEOLOGIZER

A close friend's child is dying of cancer. You are sitting next to your friend in the hospital, staring at the dying child. What will you do or say?

Has God ever *not* been there when you needed him?

TWISTER #91

Would you fudge when filling out your income tax return on items difficult for the IRS to detect? Why or why not?

TWISTER #92

THEOLOGIZER

As an alternative to life imprisonment, should convicts have the right to take their own lives with the help of the state?

Is the death penalty moral? How about the death penalty for convicted murderers who are minors?

TWISTER #93

Your teenage child asks if you ever had any sexual involvement before you were married. What will you say?

TWISTER #94

Is it morally right for Christian parents to try selecting the sex of their child?

TURN-A-BOUT

How about choosing the sex of children through selective abortion?

THEOLOGIZER

If we choose the sex of children, are we playing God?

TWISTER #95

The mechanic who repaired your car said it would run fine for another month or two but then would need major repairs. Do you sell it without mentioning this fact to potential buyers?

TWISTER  #96

A close friend said she witnessed an exorcism where a demon came out of a woman. She really believes it happened and now believes in demon possession. Do you believe her story?

TEASER

How real is Satan to you?

THEOLOGIZER

Can Satan keep you from a relationship with God if you really want one?

TWISTER #97

Your 17-year-old daughter purchased a hard rock compact disc. Overhearing the music, you are disturbed by a song's sexually permissive theme. How will you respond?

TURN-A-BOUT

What if it were your 17-year-old son?

TWISTER #98

You move into a new apartment and discover that the pay cable television is working. Do you use it for free without informing the cable company? Why or why not?

TWISTER #99

What would you do if you found out you had somehow contracted AIDS?

THEOLOGIZER

Is AIDS a curse from God?

TWISTER PLUS

What should society do for infants with AIDS?

TWISTER # 100

An elderly couple whom you have known for some time believes their useful years are past. They wish to "die with dignity" rather than suffer with ill health and a meaningless life. They have chosen to kill themselves. What would you say to them?

TEASER

Have you ever felt so overwhelmed with problems that you wished you were dead?

THEOLOGIZER

What do you think God would say about suicide?

TWISTER #101

An employee leaving your department has asked you as department head to write her a recommendation for a new job. Although you like her as a person, her work is below average. Will you write her a recommendation?

TWISTER #102

You back into someone's car at the mall. The damage is barely noticeable. How will you respond?

TWISTER # 103

TURN-A-BOUT

If you had the opportunity to save $275 on an airline ticket for your child, would you shave a year off his or her age?

What if it were to save you four dollars on dinner at a restaurant?

TWISTER #104

If evidence were found on old papyrus fragments indicating a fifth gospel with additional sayings of Jesus Christ, would you want to read them?

TURN-A-BOUT

Should this fifth gospel be added to the Bible?

TWISTER #105

A relative works at a discount department store. With his employee's discount he can get merchandise at a significant savings. Would you ask him to use his discount to help you make a major purchase?

TWISTER #106

Should the name, address, and medical history of a surrogate mother, sperm donor, egg donor, or embryo donor be made accessible to the child when she or he turns eighteen?

TEASER

You are asked to be an egg or sperm donor for a couple who cannot have children. Will you donate? What would it take for you to become a donor?

THEOLOGIZER

Is our reproductive technology surpassing our ability to handle it morally?

TWISTER PLUS

Should the names of the birth mother and father be given to an adopted child when he or she turns eighteen?

TWISTER #107

On several occasions during staff meetings, your boss has taken credit for your ideas. Will you challenge your boss? Why or why not?

TWISTER #108

A friend's child is acting up. The reason is obvious to you—it is the way your friend is raising the child. Will you say something to your friend?

TURN-A-BOUT

Would you want your friend to say something to you if the situation were reversed?

TWISTER #109

As a secretary, you are frequently required by your boss to inform callers of his absence from the office when, in reality, he is in. Does this bother you? What will you do?

TWISTER #110

TURN-A-BOUT

When a sexual aphrodisiac (a drug that arouses sexual desire) is available in drug stores, will you take it?

Would you sneak it into someone's coffee?

TWISTER # 111

TURN-A-BOUT

A couple you have been best friends with for ten years announce their divorce. Will you maintain your close relationship with both of them?

If the husband asked you to testify on his behalf in the couple's child custody hearing, would you?

TWISTER #112

As a juror hearing a criminal case, you are told by the judge to disregard an important piece of testimony. This testimony, stricken from the court record, implicates the defendant, an alleged rapist. If you ignore the testimony, the defendant will most certainly be found innocent. If you consider the testimony, you will find the defendant guilty. What will you do?

TWISTER PLUS

How "just" is the American justice system?

TWISTER #113

If a drug were invented that had no harmful side effects, was non-addictive, legal, and able to give you an incredible sense of euphoria for an hour, would you take it? Why or why not?

TWISTER #114

This is the second time you have been passed over for a raise. Do you continue to give your best to your job even though the pay is low? Explain your answer.

TWISTER #115

Amniocentesis has revealed that your unborn baby has Down's syndrome and will be born severely retarded. The doctor has recommended an abortion. What will you do?

TEASER

If you could change the abortion law, how would you change it?

THEOLOGIZER

Does God see abortion as wrong, no matter what the circumstances?

TWISTER PLUS

Would your views on abortion change if your daughter were getting the abortion?

TWISTER # 116

Your ex-spouse is suing you for an increase in child support. You feel you are paying a more than adequate amount. What do you do?

TWISTER #117

You have been invited to a party thrown by someone in your office. You discover a group of coworkers watching an X-rated porno flick on the VCR. They ask you to join them. What will you do?

TURN-A-BOUT

What would you have done if your coworkers had been smoking marijuana?

THEOLOGIZER

Was your response to the porno flick a Christian one? How about to the drug usage?

TWISTER # 118

What would need to happen for you to consider taking your mother-in-law and father-in-law into your home to live with you?

TWISTER # 119

You discover an acquaintance's 16-year-old daughter is using birth control pills. Do you tell her parents?

TURN-A-BOUT

If your teenage daughter were prescribed birth control pills to regulate her period, would you consent to filling the prescription?

TWISTER #120

Your pastor asked you to leave the church because he disagreed with the way you taught a Sunday school class. What will you do?

TEASER

What will people remember most about your church after its doors are closed?

THEOLOGIZER

What do you think the apostle Paul would say about the state of your church?

TWISTER #121

TEASER

You are asked to put together a sex education program for your church youth group. What topics would you include in your program? What ages?

If you provide sex education for young people, are you promoting premarital sexual behavior?

TWISTER # 122

TURN-A-BOUT

Would you report a coworker you know is abusing drugs?

If you were accused of using drugs by a fellow employee, would you submit to a company-required drug test?

TWISTER #123

When you first married, you shared your spouse's views about not having children. As you have grown older, your desire to have a child has grown, but your spouse has not changed. Will you stop using birth control without telling him?

TWISTER # 124

TURN-A-BOUT

The person behind the counter rings up a lower price than you figured for your lunch. Do you point out the possible mistake?

Would you have made the same choice if the clerk had rung up a higher price than you figured?

TWISTER #125

TURN-A-BOUT

Your church is boycotting and picketing a convenience store because it sells pornography. Will you participate?

How about if your church were protesting at a nuclear weapons storage facility?

TWISTER #126

Your seventy-five-year-old grandmother is in a coma. She may or may not survive it. She drew up a "living will," a document in which she requested her life not be prolonged through the use of extraordinary means. As a family member, the doctor has asked for your input. Should the respirator be removed and your grandmother allowed to die?

THEOLOGIZER

Because medical doctors have the technology and ability to extend life, does that mean it should be done?

TWISTER PLUS

How should a Christian respond to the wishes of terminally ill medical patients?

TWISTER #127

TURN-A-BOUT

A friend calls with a request to be bailed out of jail for blocking the entrance to an abortion clinic. Will you help?

The next time your friend goes to an abortion clinic to protest, will you go along?

TWISTER #128

TURN-A-BOUT

It is rainy and cold. The only available parking space close to the post office entrance is one marked for handicapped drivers. Assuming you are not handicapped, will you park there?

Would you say something to a non-handicapped person parked in a marked handicapped zone?

TWISTER # **129**

THEOLOGIZER

The monthly pledge you made toward your church's building program is more of a financial hardship than you expected. What will you do about your pledge?

What does your response say about your faith?

TWISTER # 130

TEASER

Should Christians conduct a funeral for a miscarried fetus? How about for an aborted fetus?

Thomas Aquinas, a medieval theologian, believed a male received his soul forty days after conception, a female in eighty days. When do you believe a person receives a soul?

TWISTER # 131

The one Sunday you bring a skeptical friend to church, the pastor pleads for more money. How will you explain your pastor's behavior?

TWISTER # 132

You are confronted at the entrance to a grocery store by a homeless woman with her three children, asking for help. How will you respond?

TURN-A-BOUT

If you took this homeless family to your church worship service, how would the congregation respond?

TWISTER #133

TURN-A-BOUT

You see your daughter's eighth-grade science teacher on TV as the spokesperson for the gay rights coalition in your community. How will you react? What, if anything, will you do?

You are the principal of a middle school in need of a science teacher. The most outstanding candidate for the job reveals he is a homosexual. Will you hire him?

Quickie TWISTERS

TWISTER # 134

What could you very easily become addicted to?

TWISTER # 135

What is one thing that is not a crime but you feel should be?

TWISTER #136

Is today's American church more of an aquarium keeper or a fisher of men and women?

TWISTER #137

Would your thirty-eight-year-old self disapprove of your eighteen-year-old self? Would your eighteen-year-old self approve of your thirty-eight-year-old self?

TWISTER #138

Why do people believe "it" will not happen to them?

TWISTER #139

In order to have a good time, how often do you miss sleep, eat badly, or live dangerously?

TWISTER # 140

God has issued you a one-year permit to rid one ill from our society. What ill will you choose to tackle? How will you go about tackling it?

TWISTER # 141

Is there such a thing as too much of a good thing?

TWISTER # 142

If youth is wasted on the young, is wisdom wasted on the aged? Explain.

TWISTER # 143

Are the adolescent years really the best years of life? Why or why not?

TWISTER # 144

What is meant by the saying "a clear conscience is the best pillow"?

TWISTER # 145

Is there such a thing as Christian politics? Christian public policy? Christian foreign policy?

TWISTER #146

What is a dangerous trend you see occurring in society?

TWISTER #147

How much of your time does God deserve? Explain.

TWISTER #148

What is one thing you wish had never been invented? One thing not yet invented but you wish would be invented?

TWISTER #149

Who is one of your biggest heroes or heroines?

TWISTER # 150

Must an individual lead a moral life to be happy? To be successful?

TWISTER # 151

How can a Christian be certain which interpretation of a passage of Scripture is correct with so many interpretations being offered?

TWISTER #152

What problem can technology never solve?

TWISTER #153

What is an adequate yearly income?

TWISTER #154

If you were given the choice between being a moderately happy multimillionaire or an extremely happy person living in poverty, which would you choose?

TWISTER #155

What kind of reputation do you have with people who are not Christians? What do Christians think of you?

TWISTER # 156

If you were to receive one thousand dollars for every person you spoke with about Christ, would you share Christ with more people?

TWISTER # 157

Are women more exploited than men?

TWISTER #158

What would be the worst news you could hear today? How about the best news?

TWISTER #159

Do you talk too much?

TWISTER #160

What is the worst criticism you could receive?

TWISTER #161

What is the greatest compliment you could receive?

TWISTER #162

Would Christ watch as much television as you do?

TWISTER #163

Can you trust Christians more than people who are not Christians?

TWISTER # 164

How are American Christians different from Christians outside the United States?

TWISTER # 165

How has pornography become an everyday affair?

TWISTER #166

What about life makes the most sense to you? The least sense?

TWISTER #167

What is the good life?

TWISTER # 168

You are invited to talk with a group of college students about the topic of lust. What will you tell them?

TWISTER # 169

Is it more important for a mother to work or be home with her children?

TWISTER # 170

Will the divorce rate go up or down in the future?

TWISTER # 171

What do you want your children to remember most about you?

TWISTER #172

How often do you do things to please others that are not in your best interest?

TWISTER #173

What is the most illogical concept about Christianity? The most logical?

TWISTER #174

What is the worst thing that could happen to a Christian?

TWISTER #175

Would you want your daughter or son to marry someone of another race? Another faith? Another socioeconomic group? Another country?

TWISTER #176

What would it take to get you to change careers?

TWISTER #177

Why is sex often seen as synonymous with sin?

TWISTER #178

If there were a "Disciples R Us" store, what could it sell to help you be a better Christian disciple?

TWISTER #179

Will the world be evangelized by the year 2000?

TWISTER #180

What in life distracts you the most?

TWISTER #181

If God said he would change one thing about your children, what would you want him to change?

TWISTER #182

How much doubting will God tolerate?

TWISTER #183

Have you changed the world more than it has changed you?

TWISTER # 184

If you could have an emotional garage sale, what emotional issues from the past would you get rid of?

TWISTER # 185

With all the talent and wealth in the American church, why have social problems like hunger and homelessness in America not been solved?

TWISTER # 186

What is your motto for living?

TWISTER # 187

Why are things never as good or as bad as they seem?

TWISTER #188

How are you an obstacle to yourself?

TWISTER #189

Do people deserve the problems they encounter?

TWISTER #**190**

Why can't Christians agree with each other?

TWISTER #**191**

How does the Bible contradict science?

TWISTER #192

If every child were born wanted, what would the world be like?

TWISTER #193

If Jesus were to walk back through your childhood with you, what would he tell you?

TWISTER #194

What is the first thing you think of when you hear the word *Christian*?

TWISTER #195

Would you rather be able to lose twenty pounds or inherit a thousand dollars?

TWISTER # 196

Do you make more or fewer mistakes as you get older?

TWISTER # 197

Why did Christ choose to be born into and live a life of poverty?

TWISTER #198

If Christianity were a crime, would there be enough evidence to convict you? Why?

TWISTER #199

How much wealth is too much for one family? For one church? For one country?

TWISTER #200

What is one thing standing in the way of your reaching your future life goals?

TWISTER #201

If King Solomon were alive today, what advice might he give you?

TWISTER #202

What do you wish people would say at your funeral?

TWISTER #203

What surprises you the most about suffering?

TWISTER #204

Does God want Christians to focus more on the "here and now" or the "sweet bye and bye"?

TWISTER #205

Are Christians obligated to keep the Ten Commandments? How about people who are not Christians?

TWISTER #206

What is a memory you have but wish you did not? What is a memory you wish you had but do not?

TWISTER #207

What will the future be like when today's children become adults?

TWISTER #208

When did you realize you were a Christian?

TWISTER #209

Would you want your children to do the things you have done?

TWISTER #210

What are three things you can guarantee absolutely?

TWISTER #211

What are you willing to give up in order to help others? What are you not willing to give up?

TWISTER #212

If you were to place a "time capsule" in the ground that was not going to be opened for twenty years, what items representing your life would you put in it for your posterity?

TWISTER #213

At the end of your life, you and God are reviewing a photo album of your life. What will God say to you after looking at all your life pictures?